Missouri
Facts and Symbols

by Emily McAuliffe

Consultant:
Perry McCandless
Professor of History, Emeritus
Central Missouri State College
Warrensburg, Missouri

Hilltop Books
an imprint of Capstone Press
Mankato, Minnesota

Hilltop Books are published by Capstone Press
818 North Willow Street, Mankato, Minnesota 56001
http://www.capstone-press.com

Library of Congress Cataloging-in-Publication Data
McAuliffe, Emily.
    Missouri facts and symbols/by Emily McAuliffe.
    p. cm.—(The states and their symbols)
    Includes bibliographical references (p. 23) and index.
    Summary: Presents information about the state of Missouri, its nickname, motto,
and emblems.
    ISBN 0-7368-0377-7
    1. Emblems, State—Missouri—Juvenile literature. [1. Emblems, State—Missouri.
2. Missouri.] I. Title. II. Title: Missouri. III. Series: McAuliffe, Emily. States and their
symbols.
CR203.M57M33 2000
977.8'022—dc21   99–25346
                                                                                                              CIP

Editorial Credits
Damian Koshnick, editor; Heather Kindseth, cover designer; Linda Clavel, illustrator;
    Kimberly Danger, photo researcher

Photo Credits
Doris J. Brookes, 6
G. Alan Nelson, 22 (top)
G. Randall/FPG International LLC, 14
Karlene V. Schwartz, 18
Missouri Division of Tourism, 12, 16, 20
One Mile Up Inc., 8, 10 (inset)
Photo Network/Guy Bumgarner, cover
Root Resources/James Blank, 10, 22 (middle)
Unicorn Stock Photos/Tim Shippee, 22 (bottom)

Table of Contents

Iowa
MISSOURI
Nebraska
Illinois
Mississippi River
Negro Leagues Baseball Museum
Missouri River
Kansas City
St. Louis
Jefferson National Expansion Memorial
Kansas
Jefferson City
Osage River
Elephant Rocks State Park
Graniteville
Ohio River
Ozark Mountains
Kentucky
Oklahoma
Tennessee
Arkansas
Capital
City
Mountains
Places to Visit
River

Fast Facts

Capital: Missouri's capital is Jefferson City.
Largest City: Missouri's largest city is Kansas City. About 444,000 people live in Kansas City.
Size: Missouri covers 69,709 square miles (180,546 square kilometers). It is the 21st largest state.
Location: Missouri is in the central United States.
Population: 5,438,559 people live in Missouri (U.S. Census Bureau, 1998 estimate).
Statehood: Missouri became the 24th state on August 10, 1821.
Natural Resources: Missouri has lead, stone, and zinc.
Manufactured Goods: Missourians make automobiles, airplanes, spacecraft, electronic equipment, and food products.
Crops: Farmers in Missouri grow soybeans, corn, and wheat. Missouri farmers also raise cattle, hogs, and chickens.

State Name and Nickname

Missouri's state name comes from the Missouri people. This group of Native Americans was first called the Missouri by the Fox people. The name Missouri means "people with big canoes" in the Fox language. The Fox were Native Americans who lived near the Missouri people.

The Missouri River also is named after the Missouri people. The Missouri River flows southeast across the state.

Missouri's nickname is the Show-Me State. Missouri state representative Willard Vandiver created this nickname while giving a speech in 1899. The nickname reminds Missourians to know all the facts before they make a decision.

Another nickname for Missouri is the Ozark State. The Ozark Mountains cover southern Missouri. Many people hike and camp in the Ozark Mountains.

The Ozark Mountains run south from Missouri to northeastern Oklahoma and northwestern Arkansas.

7

State Seal and Motto

Missouri adopted its state seal in 1822. The seal reminds Missourians of their state's government. The seal also makes government papers official.

A shield lies in the center of Missouri's state seal. The eagle on the shield stands for the United States. A bear stands for courage. The crescent moon stands for the state's growth. The words "United we stand, divided we fall" circle the shield. This means Missourians believe in the strength of the United States. A grizzly bear stands on each side of the shield. The bears represent strength and bravery.

Missouri's official state motto also is on the state seal. The motto is "Salus Populi Suprema Lex Esto." This Latin phrase means "the welfare of the people shall be the supreme law." The motto reminds government officials to make decisions that help Missouri's citizens.

Missouri's state seal has 24 stars. Missouri was the 24th state to join the United States.

Jefferson City is the capital of Missouri. The capitol building is in Jefferson City. Government officials meet in the capitol to make the state's laws.

Missouri has had three capitol buildings. The first two capitols burned down. Workers completed the present capitol in 1917.

The current capitol building stands on a hill above the Missouri River. A dome on the building is 238 feet (73 meters) tall. A statue of the goddess Ceres (SEER-eez) stands on top of the dome. Ceres was the Roman goddess of agriculture. She stands for Missourians' hope for a good harvest each year.

Missouri officials adopted the state flag in 1913. Missouri's state flag has three horizontal stripes. The stripes are red, white, and blue like the colors of the U.S. flag. The state seal appears in the center of the flag.

The capitol is Jefferson City's most visited tourist attraction. Missouri's state museum is in the capitol.

State Bird

Missouri's legislature adopted the eastern bluebird as the state bird in 1927. This songbird lives throughout the eastern United States.

Bluebirds are named for their color. Male bluebirds are bright blue with red-brown chests. Females have paler, blue-gray feathers and red-brown chests.

Bluebirds are small songbirds. They are about 6 inches (15 centimeters) long. Their tail feathers can be 3 inches (7.6 centimeters) long.

Bluebirds lay about five light blue eggs each spring. Eggs usually hatch in 11 to 14 days. The young birds grow large enough to leave the nest within 18 to 20 days.

Bluebirds prefer open areas such as farms, orchards, and open woodlands. Missouri's farmers value bluebirds. The birds eat grasshoppers, beetles, and crickets. Many of these insects destroy crops.

Many Missourians consider the eastern bluebird a symbol of happiness.

State Tree

Officials chose the eastern flowering dogwood as Missouri's state tree in 1955. Dogwoods grow well in Missouri's mild climate. These trees grow to be about 40 feet (12 meters) tall.

Dogwood trees flower in early spring. Each flower has four white or pink petals. The center of each flower is green and yellow.

Oval-shaped leaves grow on the dogwood's flowering branches. Small, silver hairs cover the undersides of the leaves. The leaves are green in the spring and summer. In fall, the tops of the leaves turn red and orange. Bright red berries also grow on dogwood trees in the fall.

Dogwood tree bark is dark red-brown. The wood from the dogwood is hard. Some people use the wood to make strong tools such as mallets. The wood also is used to make golf clubs.

Eastern flowering dogwood trees also are called boxwoods or flowering cornels.

State Flower

In 1923, the Missouri government adopted the hawthorn blossom as the state flower. Hawthorn blossoms grow on hawthorn trees. These trees grow to be about 3 to 30 feet (.9 to 9.1 meters) tall.

Hawthorn trees bloom in the spring. Hawthorn blossoms have green-yellow centers and white or red petals. The blossoms grow to be about .5 inches (1.3 centimeters) across. The blossoms grow in clusters. Hawthorn flowers have a sweet smell.

Hawthorn trees most often are found in open fields. Thorns protect the tree from animals that might feed on the leaves and blossoms. These thorns can be as long as 3 inches (7.6 centimeters).

Hawthorn trees grow throughout Missouri. Missourians often plant hawthorn trees in gardens or parks.

Some Missourians call hawthorn trees red haw or white haw depending on the color of the blossoms.

State Animal

Missouri officials chose the Missouri mule as the state animal in 1995. For many years, Missouri was the nation's biggest producer of mules. Mules are an important part of Missouri's history.

Mules have both horse and donkey features. Only a female horse and a male donkey can mate to produce a young mule. Mules cannot reproduce themselves. Mules have long ears, short manes, and small hooves like donkeys. Mules make a braying sound like donkeys. Mules' bodies are strong like horses' bodies.

Settlers first brought mules to Missouri in the late 1820s. Farmers saw that mules were strong and could work hard. Mules helped with many parts of farm life. Missouri mules pulled pioneer wagons westward across the United States. They also helped move troops and supplies during several wars.

Some farmers in Missouri still raise mules.

State American Folk Dance: In 1995, the square dance became Missouri's official American folk dance. Many settlers enjoyed square dancing. The dance is still popular throughout the state. At a square dance, a person calls out dance steps. The dancers follow these directions.

State Fossil: Schoolchildren chose the crinoid to be Missouri's state fossil in 1989. Crinoids looked like sea stars. Crinoids lived in the ocean that covered Missouri 250 million years ago.

State Musical Instrument: The fiddle became Missouri's state musical instrument in 1987. Fur traders first brought these stringed instruments to Missouri in the 1700s.

State Tree Nut: Officials named the eastern black walnut the official state tree nut in 1990. People put black walnuts in ice cream and candy. They also grind the shells to make soft sandpaper.

Green fruit covers walnuts when they are on the tree. The black walnut grows inside the fruit.

Places to Visit

Elephant Rocks State Park

Elephant Rocks State Park is near Graniteville. The park is named for its large pink granite rocks. The rocks stand end to end and look like a train of elephants. These rocks are about 1.2 billion years old. Visitors hike around the rocks. They also learn about the history of the park.

The Jefferson National Expansion Memorial

The Jefferson National Expansion Memorial is in St. Louis. This memorial honors the pioneers who settled the West. The Gateway Arch is part of the Jefferson Memorial. The arch is 630 feet (192 meters) tall. Workers finished the arch in 1965. Visitors ride a tram to the top of the arch.

Negro Leagues Baseball Museum

The Negro Leagues Baseball Museum is in Kansas City. Visitors to the museum learn about the league and its players. Negro League teams played from 1920 until 1960. In 1945, Jackie Robinson became the first Negro League player to play for a Major League Baseball team.

Words to Know

crescent (KRESS-uhnt)—a curved shape similar to that of the moon when it is just a sliver in the sky
fossil (FAHS-uhl)—the shape of an ancient plant or animal that is preserved in the earth's crust
harvest (HAR-vist)—to collect or gather crops that are ripe
mallet (MAL-it)—a hammer with a short handle and a heavy wooden head
orchard (OR-churd)—a place where farmers grow fruit trees
tram (TRAM)—a small, boxlike car that runs on railroad tracks or a cable

Read More

Fradin, Dennis B. *Missouri.* From Sea to Shining Sea. Chicago: Children's Press, 1994.
Hintz, Martin. *Missouri.* America the Beautiful. New York: Children's Press, 1999.
Kummer, Patricia K. *Missouri.* One Nation. Mankato, Minn.: Capstone Press, 1998.
Welsbacher, Anne. *Missouri.* United States. Minneapolis: Abdo & Daughters, 1998.

Useful Addresses

Missouri State Archives
    State Information
    Center
P.O. Box 778
Jefferson City, MO 65102

Office of the Secretary of
    State
600 West Main and 208 State
    Capitol
P.O. Box 778
Jefferson City, MO 65102

Internet Sites

Missouri Facts and Figures
http://www.missouritourism.org/facts
Missouri State Symbols
http://www.50states.com/missouri.htm
State Symbols of Missouri
http://mosl.sos.state.mo.us/ofman/stsym.html

Index